A gift for:

_____

From:

_____

Parables
OF THE VINEYARD

Pamela Reeve

Photography by KIRK IRWIN

Multnomah Gifts®
a division of Multnomah® Publishers, Inc.
Sisters, Oregon

Parables
OF THE VINEYARD

© 2004 by Pamela Reeve
published by Multnomah Gifts®
a division of Multnomah® Publishers, Inc.
P.O. Box 1720, Sisters, Oregon 97759
International Standard Book Number: 1-59052-336-9

Design by Koechel Peterson and Associates, Inc, Minneapolis, Minnesota

Images ©2003 by Kirk Irwin,
www.winephotography.com

Unless otherwise indicated, Scripture quotations are from:
The Holy Bible, New King James Version
© 1984 by Thomas Nelson, Inc.
Other Scripture quotations are from:
The Holy Bible, New International Version (NIV)
©1973, 1984 by International Bible Society,
used by permission of Zondervan Publishing House
New American Standard Bible (NASB) © 1960, 1977, 1995
by the Lockman Foundation. Used by permission.
Holy Bible, New Living Translation (NLT)
©1996. Used by permission of Tyndale House Publishers, Inc. All rights reserved.

Multnomah is a trademark of Multnomah Publishers, Inc., and is registered in the U.S.
Patent and Trademark Office. The colophon is a trademark of Multnomah Publishers, Inc.

Printed in China

Library of Congress Cataloging-in-Publication Data
Reeve, Pamela.
Parables of the vineyard / by Pamela Reeve.
p. cm.
ISBN 1-59052-336-9
1. Bible. N.T. John XV, 5—Meditations. I. Title.
BS2615.55.R44 2004
242—dc22
2003021027

For Information:
MULTNOMAH PUBLISHERS, INC. • P.O. BOX 1720 • SISTERS, OR 97759

04 05 06 07 08 09—10 9 8 7 6 5 4 3 2 1 0

www.multnomahgifts.com

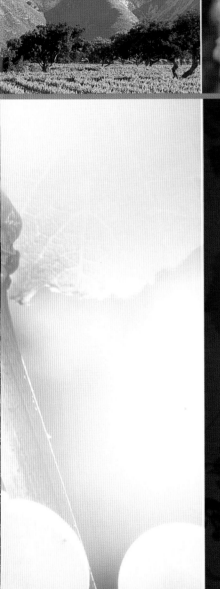

CONTENTS

Prologue
A VINEYARD

THE GREAT VINEYARD LAY BEFORE ME, AND I WASN'T IMPRESSED.

I was a young woman on my first trip to California, a state (I had been told) of wondrous and diverse beauty. But after driving many weary hours through endless miles of desert, I was beginning to wonder.

Suddenly in the midst of the sands was an impossibly large vineyard. I could hardly believe my eyes. *A vineyard? In this wasteland?* I'd just come from the East Coast, where grapevines grew on picturesque rolling green hills. This seemed too bizarre.

I turned to my mother. "This grower must be crazy—planting a vineyard in the desert. He obviously doesn't know what he's doing."

IN THE DESERT

The vines stretched on for miles, on both sides of the highway. I stopped to take a picture of this absurdity, saying to myself, *What under the sun is this? This makes no sense at all!*

Just a bit further on, we passed a massive sign:

> VIRGINIA DARE
>
> THE LARGEST VINEYARD IN THE UNITED STATES

Now I was even more surprised. I knew that name and knew it well. Virginia Dare was the premier grape of those days. For a really good product, whether it was your jams or jellies, wines or juices, all you had to do was look for the name "Virginia Dare."

I shook my head, thinking, *In the worst possible conditions, you get the most luscious grapes in the world. How can it be?*

At another time, in another season, I drove back to the vineyard. It was nearing harvest time. Stopping the car, I got out and walked among the vines. And needed no more convincing. The great clusters of deep purple and golden grapes fairly shouted the truth: The desert is a wonderful place for a vineyard.

I had much to learn about vineyards.

And about the seasons of life.

The deserts will become as green as the mountains of Lebanon,
as lovely as Mount Carmel's pastures and the plain of Sharon.
There the LORD will display his glory, the splendor of our God.

ISAIAH 35:2, NLT

Chapter 1
PLANTING

WHEREVER YOU MAY BE IN LIFE RIGHT NOW, PERSPECTIVE IS AN INVALUABLE ALLY.

In times of change, trial, disappointment, and confusion, the walls seem to close in around us. We need to know the purpose and value of the season in which we find ourselves. And we need to know that it is just that—*a season*, not a life sentence.

More important, we need to know the secret of having deep joy in the midst of any chapter in our lives—whether we're experiencing gladness or sorrow, routine or tumult.

There was a day when the disciples of the Lord Jesus were about to

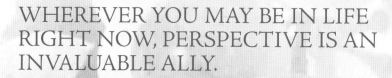

undergo a drastic change of season in their lives. They had been with the Lord through the high times, through the glory days of His great popularity and acclaim. Just four days before, they had watched a great crowd shouting, "Hosanna! Blessed is the King of Israel," as He rode into Jerusalem. They had every expectation of reigning with Him over a renewed and independent Israel. And soon.

As they celebrated the Passover meal, He warned them yet again of His coming rejection—of dark hours and dire days ahead. Paying little heed, they continued to argue about which of them would be greatest when He set up His kingdom. Jesus knew that the very next day they would see Him in agony on a cross. Then dead—and sealed in a tomb. Their expectations totally shattered, they would be hunted down,

"I am the vine, you are the branches. He who abides in Me, and I in him, bears much fruit."
JOHN 15:5

persecuted, and eventually martyred.

Catastrophic changes of season.

And Jesus gone.

They desperately needed a miracle in order to face what lay ahead. The Lord promised them that and more— unquenchable joy! He had explained it in words. Now as they walked past a vineyard, He gave them a powerful visual illustration—a word picture that would be every bit as vivid two millennia later.

The vine.

The vineyard.

It is a story for all of us, no matter where we are in life. It's about the miracle He has done in us and the secret to a life of fruitfulness— of purpose, of joy.

And of love.

Grape vines grow in a wide variety of soils, from light sand to packed clay. Before planting, the grower considers not only the soil but also the length of the season, weather conditions, fertility and drainage, topography, sun exposure, and likely pests.

You don't plant a vineyard just anywhere.

Have you ever wondered about the soil you were planted in at birth? Why God allowed you to grow up where you did?

Perhaps it was a warm, caring family who delighted in you and let you know it. Good feelings pervaded. Perhaps there was little or no nurturing or sense of security. No one let you know that you were special and loved just as you were. Tensions pervaded.

"My Father is the vinedresser," Jesus said (John 15:1). God is the grape grower. He allowed you to be planted where you were. For that matter, where you are planted *now*.

Maybe you find yourself in a place that isn't even close to what you would have expected or chosen. Perhaps it stifles any growth. Or it is an empty place, a lonely place. Or a place where many people clamor for a piece of you—your time, attention, energy—and you want out. Perhaps it is a place of aching disappointment and heartbreak over unmet expectations.

Looking back on the trials, twistings, and tragedies of your growing-up years, it may cause you to say, "It had to be a mistake! God couldn't possibly have meant me to endure what I endured."

Yet Scripture says that your Father, the Keeper of the vineyard, considered every detail—before you ever came to be. He knew what He was doing when He allowed you to grow up in your family. Looking back now, you might question His wisdom. The soil of that home may have felt like an emotional desert to you. To the untrained eye, everything looked normal. But you knew the emptiness and desolation firsthand.

On the other hand, your family soil may have been rich in love and care. Your parents delighted in you and were devoted to bringing out the best in you. It was a sunny place to be.

The Keeper of the vineyard knows how to bring forth wonderful fruit from any soil. He makes no mistake in His planting. He placed you for maximum fruitfulness.

Having planted you, He promises that He will never abandon you, never forsake you.

He knows what He is doing. He knows very well where you are planted. He knows what season it is and what season comes next. And He knows how to bring the most and the best from who you are and where you are.

Even when the vineyard is in the desert.

Chapter 2
PREPARATION

AT THE END OF THE GROWING SEASON, THE BRANCHES OF EACH GRAPE VINE HAVE AS MANY AS FIFTY TO SEVENTY OFFSHOOTS, OR CANES.

If left to themselves, they would produce upwards of 750 clusters of grapes.

An impressive number, but what sort of grapes would they be?

Poor at best. And the weight of all those clusters would weaken and eventually tear the vine—ruining many grapes.

So the canes are pruned. Severely. In fact, only *five* will be allowed to remain. This isn't like trimming a hedge; pruning takes great skill and surgical accuracy. Each cut needs to be done so as to preserve small sections of wood with a chosen number of intact buds. There isn't a random stroke in the whole process.

And pruning is part of God's work in you and me. He prunes back activities, self-seeking interests, life-sapping detours, anything that would keep us from our purpose, our one great purpose—bearing fruit.

But then there are those times—those frustrating seasons—when we are just about to become fruitful, or have already begun to see fruit in our lives, and something brings it to a halt. It feels as if we are put on a shelf—or discarded. It is a disheartening and confusing time. Even so,

God has told us He wants to give us "fruit that will last" (John 15:16, NIV). And only He knows what will last.

Sometimes He cuts our shoots back with very gentle hands. Sometimes the hands that cut aren't gentle at all—they are enemy hands.

On the night that Judas betrayed his Lord, Jesus didn't say, "The cup of suffering which Judas has given Me, shall I not drink it?" He said, "The cup which *the Father* has given Me, shall I not drink it?" (see John 18:11, NASB).

Are you going through a pruning time—a time of deep loss or wounding? God is allowing it. He uses it to accomplish some deep things in you and through you. He knows the pain and has genuine compassion. The Lord Jesus is weeping with you as He did with Mary when her brother Lazarus died.

Jesus wept with her. He groaned in His spirit with her. He understood and felt her anguish right to the bone. But He also knew what was coming, that He would soon raise Lazarus. He knew that joy and laughter and embracing were right around the corner.

What does He ask of us in the pruning times?

To submit, as Christ did, to God's agenda for our lives. To yield to the will of God, knowing that He has our highest good, our deepest joy, in mind—*though it may seem the very opposite.*

When He prunes, expect more fruit.

There is not a random stroke in His pruning.

After the pruning, each remaining cane must be tied to a supporting wire so sunlight can get to every cluster of grapes. Tying requires firm but gentle handling. Press too hard and the shoot snaps. Just that quickly, you lose one-fifth of your crop. Hold too loosely and it will spring out of your hands and hit you. It seems that some canes just don't want to stay put.

Are you tied down by circumstances out of your control? What frustration!

I think of young mothers who feel tied down by the babies in their arms and the toddlers around their feet. At the opposite end are those tied down taking care of the elderly or the chronically ill. There are so many ties that bind.

Tied down in a dull, going-nowhere job—or one filled with daily conflict and tension.

Tied down in a difficult marriage.

Tied down by the demands of extended family.

Tied down by a lingering health problem.

Tied down by advancing age and weakness.

All so limiting. And God says, "From this, I will gain much fruit."

"*Fruit?*" you answer. "But, Lord, these things are so restrictive, so confining, so frustrating. I can't go where I want to go, do what I want to do, use my talents or my experience."

The apostle John could well have felt "tied down." As John had promised Jesus at the foot of the cross that dark Friday, he was taking care of Mary, the Lord's mother…while others were doing really great things for God.

Peter, who three times denied Christ, had led five thousand to the Lord early on and opened the way to eternal life for the

Gentiles. Paul, who hadn't even known Christ during His ministry on earth, and persecuted His followers, was carrying the gospel to Turkey, Greece, and the westward frontiers. Meanwhile, ever faithful John was...well, taking care of the Lord's mother.

Oh, he did write a record of the Lord's life and ministry sometime during those years. Little did he know that millions would come to know the Lord Jesus through just one sentence he penned near the beginning of his account: "God so loved the world that he gave his one and only Son, that whoever believes in him shall not perish but have eternal life" (John 3:16, NIV). What fruit!

And in his old age, tied down in his exile to a lonely, desolate island called Patmos, he saw the glorified Christ—and an astonishing vision of the future and His triumphal reign over sorrow, sin, and death.

God does have purposes in your being tied down. Take heart, take heart. There will be fruit. It may seem unlikely, implausible, even impossible. But God ties down His vines to great effect...a harvest beyond imagination.

Chapter 3
POTENTIAL

EXCITEMENT EVERYWHERE!
"BUD BREAK" TIME!

The grower looks across his vineyard and sees life breaking forth on every hand. Sap has risen in the vine. Out of the rough and sometimes twisted old branch, tiny shoots of the bud emerge. The leaves, stems, and clusters can be seen in miniature. The persistent power of this new life flows as the vine pushes sap out to the branches. Fruit will be coming!

What a picture of the miracle Christ promised His disciples! A new life, *His* life, within them producing the fruit of His character. "Abide in Me, and I *in* you" (John 15:4). He is the One who can empower us moment by moment to be and do all that He asks. The Christian life

is not a do-it-yourself kit. He is not simply a companion walking alongside us.

This must have been as hard for the disciples to grasp as it is for us today.

It isn't simply that we have believed certain wonderful facts *about* us— that Christ died for our sins, making us right with God. It is that...and oh, so much more! A miracle has been performed *in* us. Drink this truth in. Depend on His life to make you like Him.

Do you at times feel like a rough, twisted, unsightly branch? That surely nothing of eternal value could come out of your life? There is no branch too ordinary or too warped that His indwelling life can't produce buds radiant with beauty and promise. Will you believe Him for this?

Fruit bearing is not about the branch—it's about the vine. About Christ's life in us.

The tied down, budding shoot does experience something unhampered… the sun in all its warmth and radiance, drawing it upward. Part of the Lord's lovely work is to draw us to Himself, using touches—sometimes little touches on our lives in the midst of the difficulties—to assure us of His deep love. He touches our heart, our affections, to draw us to Himself.

What is our part in all of this? We can't make ourselves bud—we can't produce life. We can't make ourselves desire Him. All we can do is what the bride in Song of Solomon did: ask and keep asking, Lord, "draw me after you" (1:4, NASB). We can learn to talk everything over with Him throughout the day, deepening our relationship with Him. We can continually remind ourselves of the awesome fact that He lives within us—*think of it!*—and keep looking to Him to supply what we need moment by moment.

He calls this abiding.

"Abide in Me, and I in you." It is depending on Him for everything, with confidence in His ever watchful care, knowing that He will hold us, cherish us, and take responsibility for the growth of our fruit. It is resting.

With this spring growth, the vineyard looks beautiful. And the life of the vine keeps thrusting its way through branch and cane in full force.

Two months after bud break, flowers begin to appear. This season is brief, the blossoms white, delicate, and lovely. The soft spring wind carries a sweet fragrance through the rows of vines. Often I'd like to stop the whole growth process right here.

But the purpose of the vine is not to produce flowers.

It is to produce grapes.

The flowers set the grapes in place. They are the size of petite peas, sour and as hard as buckshot. But everything is ready to go now. The plants have been pruned and tied. The blossoms have come and gone, and the grapes have been set in their miniature clusters. The grower can see the potential, a rich harvest, in his mind's eye and can hardly wait for it.

As God looks at you, He sees the harvest He planned to come from your life. He wants you to see it, too. Do you feel too weak or too ordinary to produce much fruit? Or that you must be confident, competent? The great secret of abiding in Christ is the realization of the indwelling Christ. It is fully accepting your weakness and believing that He will work through you in His power.

Chapter 4
DAYS OF

WE DON'T LEAP FROM SPRING-TIME TO HARVEST. NOT IN THE VINEYARD. NOT IN LIFE.

What lies between is heat.

Vines require a great abundance of sunlight because it is this heat that will eventually transform those grapes into ripe, luscious fruit. And day by day, as the path of the sun moves higher in the sky, the heat pours down. The days grow longer, and the sun burns hotter and hotter.

These are the days of stress on the vineyard.

The roots come under attack—parasite worms and insects delve beneath the soil to gnaw and consume and destroy.

TESTING

The leaves come under attack—grubs, insects, and mites descend, biting, burrowing, sapping the essential juices.

As the fruit begins to soften, the grapes come under relentless assault—raccoons, possums, and above all, birds take their toll on the immature fruit. A season of attack, yes. Yet paradoxically these are also the days when the fruit is truly formed. In our lives as believers, these are the days when all that we know about the wonderful indwelling life of Christ that would produce fruit in us is put to the test. This is the season when we learn what it means to draw upon Him as never before...as the attacks come in wave after wave.

Attacks by those who disbelieve us, disparage us, demean us, or lightly discard us.

Attacks that target all we have believed, all we have hoped and longed for—and the Lord doesn't intervene.

In these days of assault, we learn—perhaps for the first time—what it means to call upon the power of the victorious Christ dwelling within us to love our enemies.

This is where our faith in the living God gets proven. Is it real...or just a convenient accessory in our life? Is it genuine...or will it vaporize in the heat and under pressure of our testing?

We may find ourselves in places where all human love has run dry, and nothing is left. Nothing but anger and bitterness and hostility. And it is here—in this very place—that we learn to call upon Christ's life within us to produce what we could never produce in our own strength. Patience. Kindness. Perseverance. Love.

Troubles come, descending from every side—whether at home, at the office, or in those relationships that mean the most to us. Big troubles, little troubles. We find ourselves drained of emotional energy. Joy is some dim memory from the past. The tank is empty. In these difficult, dry days we learn what it means to call upon the indwelling Christ and say, *This second, Lord, this very moment, flood my heart with Your joy.*

Conflicts come, sometimes bitter and sharp, sometimes dragging on day after weary day. It takes that kind of conflict to know the peace of Jesus who lives within—not our own kind of cobbled-together peace when all is going well. When I need self-control in the face of fierce temptation, it's there—because *He* is there.

The grower has no intention of protecting his crop from this relentless heat. Even when the grape vines are tiny and newly planted, he gets heat to them by enclosing them in plastic growth tubes. These protect the young plants from insects and pests. But more particularly, they concentrate the sun directly onto the vine.

I remember feeling the testing heat four months after accepting the Lord. I had opposition at home, withdrawal from friends, and little Bible knowledge. In those days, I knew only one other person in all the world who claimed to know Christ. She'd played a part in my coming to Him.

One evening she calmly informed me that she was leaving the faith. When I tried to reason with her, she assured me that when I had gone this path for four years, as she had, my feelings would be very different.

I paced in my bedroom that night. Was she right? Was I foolish to believe all this? Crazy to follow the Lord? My heavenly Father, watching my deep struggle, gave me the conviction to say to the Lord Jesus, *I do believe in You. I don't care what she does; I am going to follow You.* In those difficult days, I came to realize that even my faith was from Him, and it "would not rest on the wisdom of men, but on the power of God" (1 Corinthians 2:5, NASB).

In a maturing vine, the leaf canopy grows dense and lush. Just when it looks like the fruit might have some relief from the incessant heat, the grower comes along and tears off leaves! If he doesn't, the interior will be dark and moist. Mildew may form, some of the bunches will not get enough sun, and some may rot. So he plucks leaves. It is said that there isn't a crop in the world that takes the constant, hands-on work that a vineyard requires.

And so it is with us, God's own choice vineyard. His hands are on us… for our good.

His hands are also placed on us to comfort and reassure. They tend the weakest tendril and the most tender shoot.

In many vineyard areas, a fog rolls in some summer evenings and lifts with the morning sun. It cools the vines during the night, protecting the leaves from burning.

So God often comes to us in the midst of the long summer with soft, cooling, comforting touches. Those intimate, tender little touches on our lives let us know that He's there, that He's watching, that He's monitoring the heat.

 During attack we have to turn to Him—cling to Him. In times such as these, times of pain, pressure, and perplexity, we need not only good understanding of His Word; we need a *Person*. We need a Person who is very present, knows precisely what's going on, and can give the compassion, strength, and support we need. We long for Someone to really understand, to encourage us. His personal presence steps out of the shadows and into our awareness. There is a joy in this deeper intimate relationship that we wouldn't trade for anything. We learn to walk in the reality of His presence. What gain!

For those grapes that are to be used for the finest purposes, the grower takes one more step. He does the thing least expected. Again, it's something that seems crazy. He purposely puts these vines under even more stress by withholding water.

The roots of the vine feel the lack of water—and the need to reduce evaporation through the leaves. They send a message to the shoot tip to stop unfolding new leaves. The shoot stops growing. No more leaves form. The energy of the vine shifts from growth to fruit ripening. And this fruit will have the best of all flavors.

Has the Lord allowed an unusual amount of stress in your life? Do you feel that everything is too much and makes no sense? That you're just trying to survive? The stressed vine produces grapes with the fine taste and rich aroma so highly valued. And it is the aroma of Christ that will attract others to Him. This is the kind of fruit He is producing in you!

Never, never forget that the Lord Jesus knows all about what you are going through. He knows those feelings. He understands the loneliness and pain. He's been there. He was stressed throughout His life and beyond imagination as He hung on the cross. There, in the face of the temptation to save Himself by coming down, He took the taunting and brutality of men and the weight of our sins, suffering the poured-out wrath of His Father and forsaken by Him.

Why? Because He loved us. "Greater love has no one than this, than to lay down one's life for his friends (John 15:13).

He says He loves us with the same intense, burning, infinite love that the Father has for *Him!*

Nothing brings such exquisite joy as knowing that love. He invites us to abide, to continually dwell in it by loving obedience to His Word. The intimacy that results will sustain us through stress and suffering.

He wants you to keep your mind, as He did, on the joy that will emerge from the sufferings of life. "Jesus…who for the *joy that was set before Him endured the cross*…and has sat down at the right hand of the throne of God" (Hebrews 12:2). Yes, and your trusting perseverence under sufferings, too, will bring a reward and a joy throughout eternity beyond your wildest imagination.

Is this the summer testing time for you? Don't give up. Don't turn away. In all the days of your life, you may never be closer to seeing His power and life flow through you. Your sense of helplessness to produce fruit will help you cling to Him in dependency. Your sense of powerlessness will cause you to call on His indwelling presence. The deepest needs of your heart will be met as you taste a love beyond telling, beyond expression.

The long hard summer of attack is really worth it.

A thousand times over.

*"Jesus…who for the joy
that was set before Him
endured the cross…and has
sat down at the right hand
of the throne of God"*

HEBREWS 12:2

Chapter 5
NEW WINE

DURING THE LAST WEEKS OF THE SEASON, THE GRAPES BEGIN TO SOFTEN AND CHANGE COLOR.

The green grapes become translucent; the red variety go from chartreuse to pink to red to purple.

Fruit is really coming!

During this time, sugar from the leaves is pumped to the grapes. The roots send water up to them, diluting their concentration of acids. Flavors begin to build. Monitoring for ripeness now takes place on a daily basis. Just the right balance of sugar and acid and the maximum amount of flavor are needed for quality grapes.

Yes, the vine is making interior changes in the fruit. And He who could cause weak, failing Peter—with some ups and downs—to stand as a rock, can change anyone.

Finally. Harvest! Celebration breaks out in the vineyard. All the vigilance, all the long hard work of the year, has been worth it. The vines may be sagging with the weight of the fruit. The remaining leaves may be dusty and wilted. The vineyard may look bedraggled. But there are the gorgeous clusters of fruit, just as they were when I walked through that vineyard in the desert so many years ago. Here are grapes that offer a lush burst of flavor as your teeth bite into them. Joy!

Harvest time speaks not only of the fruit of the Spirit in your mind, emotion, and will, but also of the fruit of your service. Nothing brings more joy than to see what God has accomplished through us in the work of the kingdom, in the lives of others.

And how God rejoices over the fruits of our service! He chose us for such fruit. Way back before there were oceans or blue skies, prairies or stars, redwood forests or fields of daisies, He planned each of us for specific tasks in His kingdom. Our service may be "a cup of cold water" to one who is in need (see Matthew 10:42), or it may be leading many to accept Christ as their Savior. The fruit in us and through us brings glory to the Father because it shows something of His character, His compassion, His immense love. Rough branches that we are, *we* bring glory to God Himself. What a privilege.

You may feel worthless and inadequate, certain that no harvest could possibly come from your life. Believe me, I know that feeling. But I have learned that the harvest does not depend on what I am, but on who He is. Look to yourself for nothing—to Him for everything. Don't ask Him to bless your best efforts, but to produce a crop through you—and in simple faith, to believe that He will.

As far as the grower is concerned, there are only two colors of grapes. Call them what you will, there are red grapes and white grapes.

I think of the red grape as a very showy kind of fruit. Some of us have showy kinds of spiritual gifts. These are the up-front people, the platform people—those who, for whatever reason, find themselves with recognizable names and recognizable faces. These are the men and women who receive attention, accolades, the limelight. God delights when the gifts He has given are well used, and He applauds along with the rest.

I think of the white grape as the less distinguished grape, hardly seen among all the leaves. These are the people who blend in, who work faithfully in the background. They perform the difficult, unseen, unapplauded, unobserved work in God's vineyard. Oftentimes, in the long run they produce the greatest amount of fruit.

God assigned your color for His purposes.

Many of us will never see the harvest we have produced. The Lord Jesus did not see the great harvest of people that would be delivered out of the kingdom of darkness and condemnation into His kingdom of love and forgiveness until after He took His place on the throne beside His Father in heaven. While on earth, He saw little result of His service. In Isaiah 49:4, we hear Him say to the Father, "I have labored in vain. I have spent my strength for nothing."

So often that can be the thought of our heart, too.

But we need to come to the same conclusion that our Lord came to in the next part of the verse: "Yet surely my just reward is with the LORD, and my work with my God." When we see no harvest from our labor, abiding means calling on the indwelling Lord for that same faith. He has promised reward—eternal reward. And He keeps His promises.

The great harvest is not the end of the season for the grower. The grapes must be picked— hot, dirty, backbreaking work if done by hand. Table grapes are loaded up for markets around the world. Juice and wine grapes, however, go to the press for crushing. The grapes are poured into the press, and unfermented juice—the new wine—pours out.

It's interesting that grape growers use the term *crush*. It brings to mind the word in

Isaiah 53:5, speaking about the Lord Jesus: "He was *crushed* for our iniquities" (NIV). His spirit was crushed within Him as He poured out His life for us in love. Crushing is not a neat surgical experience; it is brutal.

When speaking of His command to love one another, the Lord explained to His disciples what such pouring out looks like: It is laying down one's life for his friends (see John 15:13). Giving up of self and personal interests for the sake of others. Christ calls us to follow Him in this.

Much of the time that pouring out of ourselves is undramatic, unseen, sometimes unappreciated by anyone except the Father. It is, for instance:

—*a daily decision to put aside one's personal interests to meet the needs of the household.*

—*a commitment to involve oneself wholeheartedly in the interests of a spouse.*

—*caring for the needy.*

—*staying in a difficult marriage.*

—*leaving comfort and security to spread the news of God's love in faraway places.*

Laying down one's life takes thousands of forms and degrees. It is the outworking of the Vine, whose whole work is love. Pouring ourselves out for others for His sake is the path to deepest intimacy with Him.

Chapter 6

SEASONS OF

HARVEST IS OVER, BUT THE VINE CONTINUES TO GROW.

The roots still draw on the earth for nutrients; leaves still convert sunlight to carbohydrates; tiny buds prepare themselves for the following spring. In a matter of weeks, the leaves turn yellow and fall to the ground.

The vine becomes dormant.

Though there are no signs of life aboveground, the roots continue to grow through the winter.

Do you know about those dormant seasons?

Have you personally experienced those periods in life when nothing seems to be going on—when you're in the dark earth with no sense of

WAITING

warmth, no touch of the Father's love?

Conflict was better than this! And as the empty days slip by, the inevitable ponderings work their way to the surface: *Have I done something wrong? Is the Lord finished using me? After the exhilaration of the harvest, this is like having all the air sucked out of me. There may be "a future and a hope" for others, but not for me. Discouragement, despair, and the gloom of winter cover me like a dark blanket.*

What does abiding look like now?

These are the times to turn to the indwelling Lord, the God of hope, to give you hope. You can't manufacture it. You can't orchestrate it. It's time to turn to Him for the faith you need to simply trust Him—to trust that

He *does* have plans and purposes for you.

Let him who walks in the dark, who has no light, trust in the name of the LORD and rely on his God. (Isaiah 50:10, NIV)

You know at a deep level that if your life is ever to bear fruit again, it will be by His resurrection power. That you are a dead stick apart from Him.

And all the while God is doing something unseen.

Something is growing.

Something is stirring in the deep places.

He calls us to deeper trust in His plans, purposes, and character when we can't begin to trace them. Pure faith, the very root of all, is developing.

In His time, growth does begin again. The branch is stronger each year and the harvest it produces will be richer. The grower plans for cycle after cycle. The psalmist tells us that "those who are planted in the house of the LORD…shall still bear fruit in old age" (Psalm 92:13–14). For a faithful disciple of any age facing imminent death, the next cycle is heaven—a harvest of reward and joyful, fruitful service.

The secret, as one vineyard keeper put it, is to go with the cycle. Don't fight it or try to change it. Embrace it. This very season of your life—sunless and bleak as it may seem to you now—will turn, as all seasons must. And in its very turning, fresh wonders of knowing Christ will be revealed. You will taste deeper joys, glimpse higher vistas, and bring greater pleasure and glory to your God.

Yes, *embrace* the cycle.

Each cycle offers new opportunities to learn to abide, to depend on His life within for fruitfulness, to delight in His love, returning your love by obedience.

Where are you in the seasons of life right now? You, in whom God has performed the greatest of all miracles. You, who have the very life of Christ in you—a branch in the vine.

His first call to you was, "Come to Me." His second call is, *"Abide in Me."*

He wants you to bear abundant fruit so that His Father might gain glory and your joy might overflow. In heaven we will realize that the pruning, tying, attacks, and pouring out were worth it all. We will fall at the feet of the One who poured out His life's blood so that we might live forever and share His glory. Then we will sit at His table at the great marriage supper of the Lamb.

Together, with Him, we will drink of the fruit of the Vine.

I will not drink of this fruit of the vine from now on until that day
when I drink it new with you in My Father's kingdom.

MATTHEW 26:29

This is to my Father's glory,

that you bear much fruit,

showing yourselves to be my disciples.

JOHN 15:18